Women on Men 2

Compiled by
Caroline Ammerlaan

Portrait illustrations by
Rosemary Gartelmann

ISBN 0 947338 35 7

Axiom
Adelaide
South Australia

F_oreword_

Aaah! The mystery of the knowing smile, the threat of the suppressed giggle, the terrifying bravado of the outright laugh.
These were the reactions to the first volume of Women on Men: *the reactions of desperate women who've stalked the dirty sock trail and ambushed many a toilet seat left up and abandoned by its male user.*
So great was this result, the publisher has decided to present Women on Men II.
So read this volume with reverence, knowing it is dedicated to all those women living life on the edge of the bathroom.

I don't mind living in a man's world as long as I can be a woman in it.
MARILYN MONROE

Men. Difficult to love. Difficult not to.
JUDITH RODRIGUEZ

Whether women are better than men I cannot say - but I can say they are certainly no worse.
GOLDA MEIR

A man always mistakes a woman's clinging devotion for weakness, until he discovers that it requires the strength of Samson, the patience of Job, and the finesse of Solomon to untwine it.
HELEN ROWLAND

...If God had intended men to be unfaithful, he would have created two Eves.
STELLA RECAMIER

How did this notion get round that women cook only for men? Why, indeed, should we manage with some cheese just because our sexual organs are different?

ELIZABETH TAYLOR

If someone tells you he is going to make a realistic decision, you immediately understand that he has resolved to do something bad.

MARY McCARTHY

I do not wish them [women] to have power over men; but over themselves.

MARY WOLLSTONECRAFT

We were discussing the possibility of making one of our cats Pope recently, and we decided that the fact that she was not Italian, and was a female, made the third point, that she was a cat, quite irrelevant.

KATHARINE WHITEHORN

6

Every man wants a woman to appeal to his better side, his nobler instincts and his higher nature — and another woman to help him forget them.

HELEN ROWLAND

It is always incomprehensible to a man, that a woman should ever refuse an offer of marriage.

JANE AUSTEN

We learn from experience. A man never wakes up his second baby just to see it smile.

GRACE WILLIAMS

They pretend to be normal but what they're doing, sitting there with a benign smile on their faces, is they're manufacturing sperm. They do it all the time. They never stop.

GERMAINE GREER

Whenever I date a guy, I think, is this the man I want my children to spend their weekends with?

RITA RUDNER

Last night I asked my husband, "What's your favourite sexual position?" and he replied, "Next door."

JOAN RIVERS

Marriage is the deep, deep peace of the double bed after the hurly-burly of the chaise longue.

MRS PATRICK CAMPBELL

Love, the quest; marriage, the conquest; divorce, the inquest.

HELEN ROWLAND

We (women) are not more moral, we are only less corrupted by power.

GLORIA STEINEM

It requires philosophy and heroism to rise above the opinion of the wise men of all nations and races ....

ELIZABETH CADY STANTON

My mother gave me this advice: Trust your husband, adore your husband and get as much as you can in your own name.

There is a moment when a man develops enough confidence and ease in a relationship to bore you to death.

EVE BABITS

There's really nothing wrong with a woman welcoming all men's advances, as long as they are in cash.

ZSA ZSA GABOR

If the world were a logical place, men would ride side-saddle.

RITA MAE BROWN

A terrible thing happened again last night — nothing.

PHYLLIS DILLER

I wasn't allowed to speak while my husband was alive, and since he's gone no one has been able to shut me up.

HEDDA HOPPER

If man is only a little lower than the angels,
the angels should reform.

MARY WILSON LITTLE

To have a good enemy, choose a friend: he
knows where to strike.

DIANE DE POITIERS

"... it is impossible to rely on the prudence or
common sense of any man ..."

MRS ALEXANDER

I would never go to see a male gynaecologist.
That would be like having your car worked on
by a garage mechanic who never owned a car.

For though I know he loves me
Tonight my heart is sad
His kiss was not so wonderful
As all the dreams I had.

SARA TEASDALE

One cannot be always laughing at a man without now and then stumbling on something witty.

JANE AUSTEN

Men's men: gentle or simple, they're much of a muchness.

GEORGE ELIOT

If men were really what they profess to be they would not compel women to dress so that the facilities for vice would always be so easy.

MARY WALKER

Reputation is a bubble which a man bursts when he tries to blow it for himself.

EMMA CARLETON

What's the last thing a man wants to hear when he's making love?
'Hello, darling! I'm home!'

"There are some men," said Lyndall, *"whom you never can believe were babies at all; and others you never see without thinking how very nice they must have looked when they wore socks and pink sashes."*

OLIVE SCHREINER

Marrying a man is like buying something you've been admiring for a long time in a shop window. You may love it when you get it home, but it doesn't always go with every-thing else in the house.

JEAN KERR

"They forgive us—oh, for many things, but not for the absence in us of their own failings."

COLETTE

Conceding to women wisdom and goodness, as they are not strictly masculine virtues, and substituting moral power for physical force, we have the necessary elements of government for most of life's emergencies.

ELIZABETH CADY STANTON

If sex is so personal, why are we expected to share it with someone else?

LILY TOMLIN

Men may be allowed romanticism; women, who can create life in their own bodies, dare not indulge in it.

PHYLLIS McGINLEY

I did not sleep. I never do when I am over-happy, over-unhappy, or in bed with a strange man.

JANE AUSTEN

Q. Everytime I meet a man I feel my character and principles slipping from me.
A. This shows that you will succeed with men: love and business are identical, a matter of negotiation.

CHRISTINA STEAD

Only one woman in ten recognizes her husband as the same man he was before she married him. Nine out of ten say he's changed. One in three say he's changed for the worse.

GALLUP SURVEY

... money ... is really the difference between men and animals. Most of the things men feel, animals feel and vice versa, but animals do not know about money, money is purely a human conception and that is very important to know, very very important.

GERTRUDE STEIN

If it were natural for fathers to care for their sons, they would not need so many laws commanding them to do so.

PHYLLIS CHESLER

If the men in the room would only think how they would feel graduating with a 'spinster of arts' they would see how important this is.

GLORIA STEINEM

Alas, why will a man spend months trying to hand over his liberty to a woman—and the rest of his life trying to get it back again?

HELEN ROWLAND

I don't think there are any men who are
faithful to their wives.
JACQUELINE KENNEDY ONASSIS

... what is the use of being a little boy if you
are going to grow up to be a man.
GERTRUDE STEIN

I like to wake up feeling a new man.
JEAN HARLOW

17

I have always held that it was a very good thing for a young girl to fall hopelessly in love with a married man so that, later on and in the opposite predicament, she could remember what an unassailable citadel a marriage can be.

KATHARINE WHITEHORN

Seems nothing draws men together like killing other men.

SUSAN GLASPELL

In fact you expect me to submit to your unreasonableness because you haven't the courage to be honest. How like a man!

HARRIET L. CHILDE-PEMBERTON

The reason that husbands and wives do not understand each other is because they belong to different sexes.

DOROTHY DIX

*Husbands are chiefly good lovers when they
are betraying their wives.*

MARILYN MONROE

There was nothing more fun than a man!
DOROTHY PARKER

You can't change a man, no-ways. By the time his mummy turns him loose and he takes up with some innocent woman and marries her, he's what he is.
MAJORIE KINNAN RAWLINGS

Women, it is true, make human beings, but only men can make men.
MARGARET MEAD

The male sex, as a sex, does not universally appeal to me. I find the men today less manly; but a woman of my age is not in a position to know exactly how manly they are.
KATHARINE HEPBURN

How sad that men would base an entire civilization on the principle of paternity, upon legal ownership and presumed responsibility for children, and then never really get to know their sons and daughters very well.

PHYLLIS CHESLER

Changing husbands is only changing troubles.

KATHLEEN NORRIS

Man is jealous of his amour propre; woman is jealous because of her lack of it.

GERMAINE GREER

Ships at a distance have every man's wish on board. For some they come in with the tide. For others they sail forever on the horizon, never out of sight, never landing, until the Watcher turns his eyes away in resignation, his dreams mocked to death by Time. That is the life of men. Now, women forget all those things they don't want to remember, and remember everything they don't want to forget. The dream is the truth. Then they act and do things accordingly.

ZORA NEALE HURSTON

They have wonderful minds. So much is stored inside—all those sports scores and so on.

JANE SEYMOUR

There's nothing like a good dose of another woman to make a man appreciate his wife.

CLARE BOOTHE LUCE

The woman who appeals to a man's vanity may stimulate him; the woman who appeals to his heart may attract him; but it's the woman who appeals to his imagination who gets him.

HELEN ROWLAND

Men are the devil—they all bring woe.
In winter it's easy to say just "No".
Men are the devil, that's one sure thing.
But what are you going to do in spring?

MARY CAROLYN DAVIES

I have no hostility towards men. Some of my best friends are men. I married a man, and my father was a man.

JILL RUCKELSHAUS

If you want to sacrifice the admiration of many men for the criticism of one, go ahead, get married.

KATHARINE HOUGHTON HEPBURN,
mother of the actress

He was born to be a salesman. He would be an admirable representative of Rolls-Royce. But an ex-King cannot start selling motor-cars.

THE DUCHESS OF WINDSOR
(referring to her husband)

The kind of man who thinks that helping with the dishes is beneath him will also think that helping with the baby is beneath him, and then he certainly is not going to be a very successful father.

ELEANOR ROOSEVELT

Not only is it harder being a man, it is also harder to become one.
ARIANNA STASSINOPOULOS

I am a feminist because I feel endangered, psychically and physically, by this society and because I believe that the women's movement is saying that we have come to an edge of history when men—insofar as they are embodiments of the patriarchal idea—have become dangerous to children and other living things, themselves included.
ADRIENNE RICH

They say women talk too much. If you have worked in Congress you know that the filibuster was invented by men.
CLARE BOOTHE LUCE

I cannot see myself as a wife—ugly word.
GRETA GARBO

It takes a woman twenty years to make a man of her son, and another woman twenty minutes to make a fool of him.
HELEN ROWLAND

Any woman who has a great deal to offer the world is in trouble.

HAZEL SCOTT

Father asked us what was God's noblest work. Anna said men, but I said babies. Men are often bad; babies never are.

LOUISA MAY ALCOTT

There is so little difference between husbands you might as well keep the first.

ADELA ROGERS ST JOHN

Anxiety is love's greatest killer. It makes one feel as you might when a drowning man holds onto you. You want to save him, but you know he will strangle you with his panic.

ANAIS NIN

But remember, a man ends by hating the
woman who he thinks has found him out.
JENNIE JEROME CHURCHILL

"Men are like the earth and we are the moon;
we turn always one side to them, and they
think there is no other, because they don't see
it—but there is."
OLIVE SCHREINER

No matter how a man labors, some woman is
always in the background of his mind. She is
the one reward of virtue.
GERTRUDE ATHERTON

Women have changed in their relationship to
men, but men stand pat just where Adam did
when it comes to dealing with women.
DOROTHY DIX

When a man brings his wife flowers for no reason—there's a reason.

MOLLY McGEE

Fortune does not change men; it unmasks them.

SUZANNE NECKER

Learning to cherish and emphasize feminine values is the primary condition of our holding our own against the masculine principle ....

EMMA JUNG

29

*A man, it seems, may be intellectually in com-
plete sympathy with a woman's aims. But
only about ten percent of him is his intellect—
the other ninety is emotions.*

MABEL ULRICH

*Literature is strewn with the wreckage of men
who have minded beyond reason the opinions
of others.*

VIRGINIA WOOLF

It is a gentleman's first duty to remember in the morning who it was he took to bed with him.

DOROTHY L. SAYERS

The history of men's opposition to women's emancipation is more interesting perhaps than the story of that emancipation itself.

VIRGINIA WOOLF

She had always been too wise to tell him all she thought and felt, knowing by some intuition of her own womanhood that no man wants to know everything of any woman.

PEARL S. BUCK

All men are not slimy warthogs. Some men are silly giraffes, some woebegone puppies, some insecure frogs. But if one is not careful, those slimy warthogs can ruin it for all the others.

CYNTHIA HEIMEL

31

"Men ain't got any heart for courting a girl they can't pass—let alone catch up with."
JESSAMYN WEST

Most women set out to try to change a man, and when they have changed him they do not like him.
MARLENE DIETRICH

Never marry a man who hates his mother because he'll end up hating you.
JILL BENNETT

If you want anything said, ask a man. If you want anything done, ask a woman.
MARGARET THATCHER

The only time a woman really succeeds in changing a man is when he's a baby.
NATALIE WOOD

It isn't tying himself to one woman that a man dreads when he thinks of marrying; it's separating himself from all the others.
HELEN ROWLAND

Of course a platonic relationship is possible—but only between husband and wife.
LADIES HOME JOURNAL

A man in love is incomplete until he has married. Then he's finished.
ZSA ZSA GABOR

With children no longer the universally ac-
cepted reason for marriage, marriages are
going to have to exist on their own merits.
ELEANOR HOLMES NORTON

Men have always detested women's gossip be-
cause they suspect the truth: their
measurements are being taken and compared.
ERICA JONG

The first problem for all of us, men and
women, is not to learn but to unlearn.
GLORIA STEINEM

Nobody could sleep with Dick. He wakes up
during the night, switches on the lights,
speaks into his tape recorder, or takes notes—
it's impossible.
PAT NIXON

The best way to hold a man is in your arms.
MAE WEST

I only like two kinds of men: domestic and imported.

MAE WEST

Sadly, man recognises that the ideal, submissive woman he has created for himself is somehow not quite what he wanted.

EVA FIGES

I refuse to consign the whole male sex to the nursery. I insist on believing that some men are my equals.

BRIGID BROPHY

Men have laid down the rules and definitions by which the world is run, and one of the objects of their definitions is woman.

SALLY KEMPTON

No man can call himself liberal, or radical, or even a conservative advocate of fair play, if his work depends in any way on the unpaid or underpaid labor of women at home, or in the office.

GLORIA STEINEM

The man has the burden of the money. It's needed day after day. More and more of it. For ordinary things and for life. That's why holidays are a hard time for him. Another hard time is the weekend, when he's not making money or furthering himself.

GRACE PALEY

If love means never having to say you're sorry, then marriage means always having to say everything twice. Husbands, due to an unknown quirk of the universe, never hear you the first time.

ESTELLE GETTY

The usual masculine disillusionment in discovering that a woman has a brain.
MARGARET MITCHELL
Gone With The Wind

... the sexes in each species of beings ... are always true equivalents—equals but not identicals ....
ANTOINETTE BROWN BLACKWELL

Marriage, for a woman at least, hampers the two things that made life to me glorious— friendship and learning.
JANE HARRISON

If you never want to see a man again, say, "I love you, I want to marry you. I want to have children"—they leave skid marks.
RITA RUDNER

Such ignorance. All the boys were in military schools and all the girls were in the convent, and that's all you need to say about it.
KATHERINE ANNE PORTER

If you weren't such a great man you'd be a terrible bore.
MRS WILLIAM GLADSTONE
(to her husband)

Freud, of course, was wrong when he claimed that women suffer from penis envy—it is men who do.
SABRINA SEDGEWICK

Distrust that man who tells you to distrust.
ELLA WHEELER WILCOX

*If I had been born a man, I would have con-
quered Europe. As I was born a woman, I
exhausted my energy in tirades against fate,
and in eccentricities.*
MARIE BASHKIRTSEFF

*The fantasy of every Australian man is to have
two women—one cleaning and the other
dusting.*
MAUREEN MURPHY

*Man is kind only to be cruel; woman cruel
only to be kind.*
MINNA ANTRIM

*To the old saying that man built the house but
woman made of it a "home" might be added
the modern supplement that woman accepted
cooking as a chore but man has made of it a
recreation.*
EMILY POST

"... of all devils let loose in the world there (is) no devil like devoted love..."
DOROTHY L. SAYERS

Men cook more, and we all know why. It is the only interesting household task. Getting down and scrubbing the floor is done by women, or by the women they've hired.
NORA EPHRON

Probably the only place where a man can feel really secure is in a maximum security prison, except for the imminent threat of release.
GERMAINE GREER

The First Lady is an unpaid public servant elected by one person—her husband.
LADYBIRD JOHNSON

It is ridiculous to think you can spend your entire life with just one person. Three is about the right number. Yes, I imagine three husbands would do it.
CLARE BOOTHE LUCE

"... love's a nervous, awkward, overmastering brute; if you can't rein him, it's best to have no truck with him."
DOROTHY L. SAYERS

The only reason I had nine children by him is that I was hoping to lose him in the crowd.
WENDY HARMER

The hardest task in a girl's life is to prove to a man that his intentions are serious.
HELEN ROWLAND

... what is human and the same about the males and females classified as Homo sapiens is much greater than the differences.
ESTELLE R. RAMEY

If it's a woman, it's caustic; if it's a man, it's authoritative. If it's a woman, it's too often pushy; if it's a man it's aggressive in the best sense of the word.
BARBARA WALTERS

43

There is another way in which the general opinion, that women are inferior to men, is manifested ... I allude to the disproportionate value set on the time and the labor of men and women.

SARAH MOORE GRIMKE

In man, the shedding of blood is always associated with injury, disease, or death. Only the female half of humanity was seen to have the magical ability to bleed profusely and still rise phoenix-like each month from the gore.

ESTELLE R. RAMEY

We women ought to put first things first. Why should we mind if men have their faces on the money, as long as we get our hands on it?

IVY BAKER PRIEST

Women's chains have been forged by men, not by anatomy.

ESTELLE R. RAMEY

*Obtain power, then, by all means; power is the
law of man; make it yours.*
MARIA EDGEWORTH

*I have yet to hear a man ask for advice on how
to combine marriage and a career.*
GLORIA STEINEM

*If a man watches three football games in a row,
he should be declared legally dead.*
ERMA BOMBECK

Much polarity between men and women has centered around procreation. But the sex act itself is neither male nor female: it is a human being reaching out for the ultimate in communication with another human being.

DEL MARTIN

Behind every great man there is a surprised woman.

MARYON PEARSON

If divorce has increased one thousand percent, don't blame the woman's movement. Blame our obsolete sex roles on which our marriages were based.

BETTY FRIEDAN

*I think every woman is entitled to a middle
husband she can forget.*
ADELA ROGERS ST JOHN

*Men wander
Women weep
Women worry
While men are asleep*
DORY PREVIN

*All too many men still seem to believe, in a
rather naive and egocentric way, that what
feels good to him is automatically what feels
good to women.*
SHERE HITE

*In Biblical times, a man could have as many
wives as he could afford. Just like today.*
ABIGAIL VAN BUREN

I've never forgotten the first day I saw him but I'm trying hard.

There are men I could spend eternity with. But not this life.
KATHLEEN NORRIS

Jabez Hacker had one of those hard, angular natures that fitted his name like a plug of dynamite in a rock.
KYLIE TENNANT

I did have a chaperon in the US, but there was a feeling that I wouldn't need one here—perhaps because Australian men are docile.
ANN SIDNEY

The first time Adam had a chance, he laid the blame on woman.
LADY NANCY ASTOR

48

He was (so evidently) bigger than her, stronger than her, lazier than her — and are not these, in women's eyes, the three invincible marks of masculinity?

YVONNE ROUSSEAU

If you are looking for a kindly, well-to-do older gentleman who is no longer interested in sex, take out an ad in The Wall Street Journal.

ABIGAIL VAN BUREN

I think men are sex objects — because they are only good for sex and not much else.

JACKI WEAVER

... beware of men who cry. It's true that men who cry are sensitive to and in touch with feelings, but the only feelings they tend to be sensitive to and in touch with are their own.

NORA EPHRON

Marriage is a business of taking care of a man and rearing his children ....It ain't meant to be no perpetual honeymoon.

CLARE BOOTHE LUCE

If little boys have to meet and assimilate the early shock of knowing that they can never create a baby with the sureness and incontrovertibility that is a woman's birthright, how does that make them more creatively ambitious, as well as more dependent upon achievement?

MARGARET MEAD

... a woman should never use her husband as her confessor; it demands more virtue of him than situation allows.

GEORGE SAND

... I had no reason to doubt that brains were suitable for a woman. And as I had my father's kind of mind—which was also his mother's—I learned that the mind is not sex-typed.

MARGARET MEAD

A husband is what is left of the lover after the nerve has been extracted.

HELEN ROWLAND

Beware of the man who wants to protect you; he will protect you from everything but himself.

ERICA JONG

At twenty, a man feels awfully aged and blasé; at thirty, almost senile; at forty, "not so old"; and at fifty, positively skittish.

HELEN ROWLAND

The core problem women face in combining career and marriage is, quite simply, their husbands. Their husbands' attitudes. Expectations. Fears. Insecurities.

DR JOYCE BROTHERS

There is more difference within the sexes than between them.

IVY COMPTON-BURNETT

The same woman may be a goddess to a boy, a temptation to a married man, and a "menace" to a bachelor.

HELEN ROWLAND

Satan will be obliged to extend his courtyard, since men insist upon furnishing him with such quantities of paving material.

MINNA ANTRI

Men, having kept work as their exclusive pre-serve for so long, are defensive with the women who try to enter it, and show a strong tendency to shunt us into the more traditional female roles—not managing director, but his PA; not headmaster, but deputy; not sales, but personnel, and so on.

CATHY DOUGLAS

Being pertinently impertinent and properly improper has often won an impecunious man social prestige.

MINNA ANTRIM

There is perhaps one human being in a thousand who is passionately interested in his job for the job's sake. The difference is that if that one person in a thousand is a man, we say, simply, that he is passionately keen on his job; if she is a woman, we say she is a freak.

DOROTHY L. SAYERS

... we still wonder at the stolid incapacity of all men to understand that woman feels the invidious distinctions of sex exactly as the black man does those of colour, or the white man the more transient distinctions of wealth, family, position, place, and power; that she feels as keenly as man the injustice of disfranchisement.

ELIZABETH CADY STANTON

Women are not forgiven for aging. Bob Redford's lines of distinction are my old-age wrinkles.

JANE FONDA

Three wise men? You've got to be kidding!

*Men know so little about us [women]. We've
a weakness, it is true, for those who charm us,
but we always come back to those who love us.*
H. BECQUE

*A girl would feel less broken apart after a
misguided love affair if she could feel that she
had been sinful rather than a fool.*
PHYLLIS McGINLEY

*The men marry us, keep us and our children;
give us allowances, buy life insurance, and
leave us their money and even hand us ali-
mony! But all for one reason, and one reason
alone. To buy us off! They don't want us
running the world; they are willing to pay a
lot, so they can run it themselves.*

*What is man, when you come to think upon
him, but a minutely set, ingenious machine for
turning, with infinite artfulness, the red wine
of Shiraz into urine?*
ISAK DINESEN (KAREN BLIXEN)

*There are so many kinds of awful men—
One can't avoid them all. She often said
She'd never make the same mistake again:
She always made a new mistake instead.*
WENDY COPE

*It serves me right for putting all my eggs in
one bastard.*
DOROTHY PARKER

Now, we are becoming the men we wanted to marry. Once women were trained to marry a doctor, not be one.

GLORIA STEINEM

To find a rare jewel is easy.
To get a good man is harder.

YU HSUAN-CHI

Men always try to keep women out of business so they won't find out how much fun it really is.

VIVIEN KELLEMS

A Bachelor of Arts is one who makes love to a lot of women and yet has the art to remain a bachelor.

HELEN ROWLAND

It is a truth universally acknowledged, that a single man in possession of a good fortune must be in want of a wife.

JANE AUSTEN

Birth control tips. No matter how sincere those big blue eyes of his are, don't believe him when he tells you he had a vasectomy when he was sixteen.

SALLY BROWN

How is it that this world has always belonged to the men ...?

SIMONE DE BEAUVOIR

A husband is the bloke that sticks with you through the troubles you wouldn't have had if you hadn't married him in the first place.

*Time comes when every man's got to feel
something new—when he's got to feel young
again, just because he's growing old. ... A man
has only one escape from his old self: to see a
different self—in the mirror of some woman's
eyes.*

CLARE BOOTHE LUCE

*As things are, they (women) are ill-used.
They are forced to live a life of imbecility, and
are blamed for doing so. If they are ignorant,
they are despised, if learned, mocked. In love
they are reduced to the status of courtesans.
As wives they are treated more as servants
than as companions. Men do not love them:
they make use of them, they exploit them, and
expect, in that way, to make them subject to
the law of fidelity.*

GEORGE SAND

*There are not many males, black or white, who
wish to get involved with a woman who's
committed to her own development.*

ELEANOR HOLMES NORTON

*Men define intelligence, men define useful-
ness, men tell us what is beautiful, men even
tell us what is womanly.*
SALLY KEMPTON

*A man is allowed to blaspheme the world
because it belongs to him to damn.*
SHULAMITH FIRESTONE

*'I got a pair of socks for my husband.'
'Dammit, I wish I could swap mine for something useful.'*

It is funny the two things most men are proudest of is the thing that any man can do; and doing, does in the same way, that is being drunk and being the father of their son.
GERTRUDE STEIN

I believe in the single standard for men and women.
MAE WEST

... men want recognition of their work, to help them to believe in themselves.
DOROTHY MILLER RICHARDSON

Man's role is uncertain, undefined, and perhaps unnecessary. By a great effort man has hit upon a method of compensating himself for his basic inferiority.
MARGARET MEAD

Man, in conquering nature, conquered the female, who had worked with nature, not against it, to produce food and to reproduce the human race.
ROXANNE DUNBAR

More husbands would leave home if they knew how to pack.

Women, however, as the bearer and guardian of the new lives, have everywhere greater respect for life than man, who for centuries, as hunter and warrior, learned that the taking of lives may be not only allowed, but honourable.
ELLEN KEY

As long as you know that most men are like children you know everything.
COCO CHANEL

Women fail to understand how much men hate them.
GERMAINE GREER

Are there any brothers who do not criticize a bit and make fun of the fiance who is stealing a sister from them?
COLETTE

I don't consider the Equal Rights Amendment a political issue. It is a moral issue as far as I am concerned. Where are women mentioned in the constitution except in the Nineteenth Amendment, giving us the right to vote? When they said all men were created equal, they really meant it—otherwise, why did we have to fight for the Nineteenth Amendment?
CAROL BURNETT

Call no man foe, but never love a stranger.
STELLA BENSON

*Men are taught to apologize for their weak-
nesses, women for their strengths.*
LOIS WYSE

*Where's the man could ease a heart like a satin
gown?*
DOROTHY PARKER

*A self-made man is one who believes in luck
and sends his son to Oxford.*
CHRISTINA STEAD

*I am more and more convinced that man is a
dangerous creature....*
ABIGAIL ADAMS

Most men want their wives to have a jobette.
GLORIA STEINEM
quoting a woman criminal lawyer

If a man fights his adversaries, he's called determined. If a woman does it, she's frustrated.

ESTHER PETERSON

He's the kind of bore who's here today and here tomorrow.

BINNIE BARNES

No man knows his true character until he has run out of gas, purchased something on the installment plan and raised an adolescent.

MERCELENE COX

And you're not going to have a society that understands its humanity if you don't have more women in government.

BELLA ABZUG

Failing to be there when a man wants her is a woman's greatest sin, except to be there when he doesn't want her.

HELEN ROWLAND

The head never rules the heart, but just becomes its partner in crime.
MIGNON McLAUGHLIN

Almost all married people fight, although many are ashamed to admit it. Actually a marriage in which no quarrelling at all takes place may well be one that is dead or dying from emotional undernourishment. If you care, you probably fight.
FLORA DAVIS

Be kind to animals—kiss a man today.

Men say they love independence in a woman, but they don't waste a second demolishing it brick by brick.
CANDICE BERGEN

*Sure God made man before woman, but then
you always make a rough draft before the final
masterpiece.*

He eats like a horse afire.
ANGELINA BICOS

*Beware of the man who praises liberated
women; he is planning to quit his job.*
ERICA JONG

My husband doesn't munch words!

MARY CARTER

*There are poor men in this country who can-
not be bought: the day I found that out, I sent
my gold abroad.*

COMTESSE DE VOIGRAND

Thomas Wolfe has always seemed to me the most overrated, longwinded and boring of reputable American novelists.

EDITH OLIVER

Success has made failures of many men.

CINDY ADAMS

I don't mind being a grandmother, but I object to going to bed with a grandfather.

ANONYMOUS

A woman fit to be a man's wife is too good to be his servant.

DOROTHY LEIGH

Why are blonde jokes so simple?
So men can understand them.

A woman despises a man for loving her,
unless she returns his love.
ELIZABETH DREW STODDARD

Any one must see at a glance that if men and
women marry those whom they do not love,
they must love those whom they do not marry.
HARRIET MARTINEAU

It is possible for a woman to love a man—but
only if she doesn't know him very well.

Man in his lust has regulated long enough
this whole question of sexual intercourse.
Now let the mother of mankind, whose
prerogative it is to set bounds to his
indulgence, rouse up and give this whole
matter a thorough, fearless examination.
ELIZABETH CADY STANTON

A bachelor is a man who is right sometimes.
BARBRA STREISAND

A woman has to consider whether her dress is too short, her trousers too tight, her V neck too low, whether her legs are shaved, her lipstick is on right, whether her hair looks best up or down. A man makes sure his zipper is closed and gets on stage.

RACHEL BERGER

I gave my beauty and my youth to men. I am going to give my wisdom and experience to animals.

BRIGITTE BARDOT

Wealth makes them lavish, with knavish, beauty effeminate, poverty deceitful, and deformity ugly. Therefore, of me take this counsel:
Esteem of men as of a broken reed, Mistrust them still, and then you well shall speed.

JANE ANGER

Men are frustrated when their sincere attempts to help a woman solve her problems are met not with gratitude but with disapproval. One man reported being ready to tear his hair out over a girlfriend who continually told him about problems she was having at work but refused to take any of the advice he offered.

DEBORAH TANNEN

In olden times, sacrifices were made at the altar—a practice which is still continued.

HELEN ROWLAND

Women are brighter than men. That's true. But it should be kept very quiet or it ruins the whole racket.

ANITA LOOS

When women go wrong, men go right after them.

MAE WEST

Sylvia said, 'Men are stronger than women. They don't need such complete rest.' Kimi said, "Nonsense, it is because the Medical Director is also a man. He thinks, "The woman's mind is little. She can lie twenty-four hours a day for thirty days, a total of seven hundred and twenty hours, doing nothing. The man's mind is big. He must give it something to think about. I will let him read the paper immediately."'

BETTY MacDONALD

Women have moved and shaken me, but I have been nourished by men.

MAY SARTON

Men think monogamy is something you make dining room tables out of.

KATHY LETTE

A successful man is one who makes more money than his wife can spend. A successful woman is one who can find such a man.

LANA TURNER

*Nothing could be more grotesquely unjust
than a code of morals, reinforced by laws,
which relieves men from responsibility for
irregular sexual acts, and for the same acts
drives women to abortion, infanticide,
prostitution and self-destruction.*
SUZANNE LAFOLLETTE

*Fighting is essentially a masculine idea; a
woman's weapon is her tongue.*
HERMIONE GINGOLD

Sexiness wears thin after a while and beauty fades, but to be married to a man who makes you laugh every day, ah, now that's a real treat!

JOANNE WOODWARD

Choose a slow lingering death. Get married.

Love will never be ideal until man recovers from the illusion that he can be just a little bit faithful or a little bit married.

HELEN ROWLAND

No one should have to dance backwards all their lives.

JILL RUCKELSHAUS

The world cannot do without women, which is why there's resentment from men. They realise the future lies with us.

JOAN COLLINS

When a man is alone he's mighty apt to be with the devil—if he ain't with God. He has to choose which company he'll keep, I reckon.

LUCY MAUD MONTGOMERY

It's better to learn to say good-by early than late.

JESSAMYN WEST

He who hesitates is last.
MAE WEST